A BINARY HEART

stories by

DS Levy

Finishing Line Press
Georgetown, Kentucky

A BINARY HEART

ACKNOWLEDGMENTS
Some of these stories were published in slightly different form in the following:

"There Once Was a Girl," *FewerThan500.com*
"Moving Day," *The Molotov Cocktail*
"Friend Mildred," *Clever Magazine*
"A Binary Heart" (originally titled "A Vacuum Abhors"), *101 Words*
"Milk," Micro Text Anthology, *Medusa's Laugh Press*
"The Deep End," *South Dakota Review*
"Mr. Doolittle," *Corvus Review*
"Another Life," *Brilliant Flash Fiction*
"Button, Button," *SUNDOG* (World's Best Short-Short Story Contest, Finalist, 1996)
"At the Beach," *Cleaver Magazine*
"Museum Pieces," *Columbia: A Journal of Literature & Art*
"Paper Cup," Every Day Fiction
"E-Book Discussion Questions (A Sample)," *Cease, Cows*
"Some Numbers" and "Jackpot," *Brevity*
"Your Heartbeat," *Boston Literary Magazine*

I would like to thank Finishing Line Press for making this chapbook possible.

I would also like to thank the talented writer and artist AM Roselli for her stunning
artwork and perceptive editing eye, and most of all for sprinkling her Italian pixie dust on
these stories making them infinitely stronger (*Grazie mia cara amica per avermi aiutato a
governare la barca a riva.*).

Special hugs to Charlie & Company for unconditional love, as well as for teaching me the
value of sitting and staring out the window. And loving thanks to my husband, Bob, for
always supporting me and my writing—though a non-dancer, your astute reading of these
stories saved me from publicly stepping on my own two feet.

Publisher: Leah Maines
Editor: Christen Kincaid
Cover Art: AM Roselli, "Bare Back"
Author Photo: Jesse Pennington
Cover Design: Elizabeth Maines McCleavy

Printed in the USA on acid-free paper.
Order online: www.finishinglinepress.com
        also available on amazon.com

Author inquiries and mail orders:
Finishing Line Press
P. O. Box 1626
Georgetown, Kentucky 40324
U. S. A.

Table of Contents

for mom and dad

THERE ONCE WAS A GIRL

Her grandmother always said—*Eat, you need to eat.*

At night the girl dreamt the craziest things and in the morning she'd wake and eat them for breakfast. Nocturnal bonbons and phantasmagorical sticky buns with caramel glazing went down easily and digested so well she couldn't wait to get up and greet the day. But dreams weren't the Breakfast of Champions, and the AMA refused their seals of approval. The girl could have done worse.

She could have eaten her worries, like her own dear mother who, gaunt and aged before her years, bemoaned every last trouble she'd ever put to her lips. "Yes," the girl said to her sullen mother one morning, "I've heard that worries are foul-tasting, every bit as tough as shoe leather. No wonder you're not putting any weight on." But her mother wouldn't listen and continued to chew worries that came her way because they were all she had to eat—and besides, all she'd ever dreamt were nightmares which left a terrible aftertaste.

And then there was the girl's father who feasted on reality which sometimes was quite delectable but mostly quite dismal. His face was ashen and his shoulders stooped from holding realities as he nibbled them like ears of corn. Even though he ate them with a little butter and salt, his realities never lived up to expectations. The mother had eaten all the worries about imitation spreads and kept only real butter churned out from the farmer down the road. Still, nothing satisfied either of them.

After some time the mother grew so thin that when she turned sideways the girl and her father couldn't see her. And the father became so bent over and his skin so transparent he was nearly invisible to the girl and her mother. But the little girl was flourishing. She couldn't wait to go to bed when the sun went down and to get up when it rose again.

*

Years later, the girl turned from dreams to words, which sustained her when she might have starved. Some were tasty, others despicable. So many words, so little time—and her arthritic fingers plink-plinked across the keyboard.

As they say, we feed ourselves with what we have.

RE:

I was thinking it might be nice if you reloved me. You'd have to release all that bitter angst from your heart and stop accusing me of any repugnant behaviors you claim I possess. You would need to reload affection before releasing regret and reacquaint yourself with our memories of the past, readdressing them in the present, which you would have to redefine, releasing any hard feelings, of which there were many. We would have to redact bitter words and biting conversations. At the very least, we would have to reavow what had once been embedded in our hearts.

MOVING DAY

The Braddocks were moving.

Brenda Hanson stood at the upstairs window, spying through parted blinds. Down on the street, Melissa and Bill Braddock oversaw three young, shirtless men who were easing the Braddocks' covered furniture and boxes into a moving truck. The sun was bright and the reflection off the sparkling cement hurt Brenda's eyes.

Brenda was appreciative of her temporary discomfort. Melissa Braddock had been blinded in a car accident years ago—long before the Braddocks had moved into the resort. But Melissa hardly ever needed her husband to escort her around—like a blind person, Brenda was thinking.

The movers had smooth dark tans, muscled arms. Two of them Brenda recognized as former high school football players. They'd been minor celebrities in the small town. She didn't recognize the other one.

"Do you want croutons?" Jim yelled up from the kitchen. The Hansons had screamed at each other like this for years. They never seemed to be in the same room at the same time.

"No," Brenda called down.

"Well, lunch is ready then." Since his retirement last year, Jim had become the *Chef de cuisine*, which was fine with Brenda. She'd never been much of a cook.

Melissa Braddock on the other hand was a gourmet chef. She had a professional chef's kitchen and knew where every fork, knife, spoon and spatula belonged. She even sliced her own onions.

"Should she be doing that?" Brenda had whispered to Bill the day she'd gone over to welcome them to the resort. The three of them were standing in the kitchen, and Bill Braddock said there was nothing to worry about, his wife had never once cut herself.

The Braddocks' townhouse was a mirror image of the Hansons', except for the layout, which was flipped so that Brenda had had a slight discombobulated feeling when she'd first walked in. She'd told Bill she liked the way they'd decorated with nautical adornments, and Bill told her it was all Melissa's doing.

"Really?"

"Yes, despite her situation my wife has a wonderful eye for decorating."

"You're making me blush," Melissa Braddock said to her husband, dumping the onions into a pot on the stove.

"And cooking," Brenda added.

"That too," he said, and then slowly wagged his tongue at Brenda once, and then once again. The gesture had so surprised Brenda she was certain she'd imagined it and rubbed her left eye. But a few seconds later Bill Braddock did it again, this time the provocation undeniable.

Brenda excused herself, told the Braddocks her husband was waiting for her so they could go to the marina and wash down the sailboat. Just then Melissa pulled a cherry pie out of the oven, holding the steaming pastry with fireproof gloves. The filling bubbled up through the slits in the golden crust. Melissa said, "Why don't you take a couple slices home with you, we have plenty?"

But Brenda said her husband was diabetic and once had even ended up in the hospital. "He has absolutely no willpower," she said. "He'd eat both pieces, and there'd go his sugar, spiked to heaven." In fact, she had fabricated the entire disease.

Melissa frowned, told Brenda how sorry she was to hear that. Her eyes seemed to focus straight-ahead, on the kitchen wall. Brenda let herself out and hurried home.

From that day forward Brenda never went down to the Braddock townhouse without Jim at her side. A couple of times the Braddocks had invited them to play bocce ball, which Melissa was evidently quite good at, but Brenda had given the excuse that she was no good at games, which was not altogether a lie.

They had begged off, so what?

Now the Braddocks were moving and Brenda watched Bill Braddock guide his wife back into the empty townhouse. She saw Bill's dull, dead eyes and his wife's distant face.

FRIEND MILDRED

December 9, 1915

Friend Mildred,
A view of a town in Germany that we passed through on our march.
We also spent the night at this town. I am on the sick list at the
present time, but not at the hospital.
Yours truly,
Louis

     Mildred Anderson was an only child who lived with her mother. By age twenty, girls were married and most were already pregnant with their second child, but Mildred was 46, far beyond her prime. She was too old to be wooed by a man, especially one fighting the Good War overseas. Still it had been kind of him to call her "friend."

     She'd only been doing her part, serving her country. The women in her church had come up with the letter-writing campaign. She'd never expected to get anything in return. His postcard had come in the mail. A bright spot lying on the dark kitchen table, postmarked December 22, 1915. Gerolstein, Germany appeared to her an odd mixture of stone castles and lush vegetation set against a backdrop of what could only be said to look like the US Western plains—which Mildred knew from photos. She'd never been farther than the Mississippi River. The area didn't look dangerous, there were no rifles, machine guns or bayonets as she'd read about, no troops in deep dirt trenches. It was nice to pretend there was no dying.

She held the postcard to her nose. It smelled like ink. She hoped Louis was feeling better by the time he had sent it, and that he'd gotten a good night's sleep. She wondered why he was on the sick list but not in a hospital. How sick did one have to be to get a hospital bed? Maybe he had a common cold and was in need of warm socks.

She imagined him reading her letter, which she had composed on scrap paper then copied to clean stationery. Was he tall and thin with warm penetrating eyes, or short and solid with a reliable chin, square and true? Maybe he had nice wavy hair like Charles Chaplin.

She fancied he'd had similar questions about her as his hand tracked across the back of the postcard leaving kind words in red ink. His penmanship was the mark of a serious man, each letter laid down with tight precision. Did he carry thoughts of her with him as he and his regiment marched through the small German town into the surrounding mountains and on into battle?

She touched the postcard to her dry lips imagining the lingering traces of genteel fingertips. Though she was as plain as the postcard's washed out golden sky, he'd taken the time to write. He had been kind enough to call her "friend." Friend Mildred. She hoped he had several pairs of good, warm socks. Sometimes warm socks were closer to God than heart-felt caresses. It was nice to pretend.

A BINARY HEART

I must admit, I miss you. Somewhere out there in the black of night in binary combinations that can't be fathomed, I stumble the distance, searching. My fingers turn over rocks and words—either will sink. I hold on, floating in brackish waters darker than your eyes. It's funny that I should seek what I abhor. But isn't that always the way? Don't we rush to judgment too soon? Don't we go looking for hearts darker than our own? And when we find them aren't we always just a little bit thrilled until the tide of regret washes over us?

MILK

The child kept the woman up all night longing for milk the woman did not have. She did not have milk but she had a headache from listening to the screaming child, a cacophony so intense neighbors—the woman lived in an apartment—pounded on the floor and ceiling, and the woman herself liked to have gone back to Symphony Hall, where earlier in the evening she had been listening to a famous violinist play a little-known Bach concerto, which was the woman's favorite piece of music. Though the tickets had been expensive and difficult to obtain, she had been lucky enough to get one. One thing she forgot to get, however, was a babysitter for the child, whom she apparently thought was old enough to amuse itself with fish, a whole school of beautiful gold and silver minnows dangling languidly from a mobile bought that morning. That night, punch-drunk on Bach, the woman came home to find the mobile standing still and a red-faced child screaming. She knew immediately what she must do: hurry to the store for some milk. Milk she could not provide herself, since earlier that morning while passing through the park she had stolen the sleeping child from its mother who, only a few minutes before, had calmed the screaming infant and who herself slept peacefully under the soft, enveloping arms of a maple tree, tender breasts no longer engorged.

THE DEEP END

That night my father was in the pool at the Pink Flamingo Motel. He was swimming backwards in the deep end, showing off for my mother and me. He was old enough to be my grandfather, is what I was thinking as I watched him propel himself from side to side, matching my breath to his.

He had a nice backstroke. His movement was fluid, efficient. In the pool he looked young, trusting the water to buoy his rigid body. Nevertheless, he made me nervous down there in the deep end.

My mother and I were squatting in the shallow end, huddled beside the underwater floodlight we told ourselves was heating the water. As long as the surface remained calm the water seemed warmer. And as long as I didn't look at the goosebumps on my mother's white thighs, magnified where light and liquid came together, it was easy to believe.

"Hello, girls," my father called out from the deep end.

"Hello, yourself," my mother said, turning her neck slowly to track his progress. She held her head high above the water to keep from getting her new hair color wet. Before we'd left on vacation, she had switched from Autumn Blond to Fabulous Fawn, and already she was having her doubts. She didn't want to compound the problem with chlorine.

"I'm getting out," she said.

"Come on down where the water's wet," my father said, treading above the drain pipe.

"I've had enough," she said, then looked at me. "Coming?"

We water-walked across the shallow end to the cement steps that fanned out scallop-like underwater. My mother pulled her leg out, making a splash that was the first either of us had managed that evening.

From the deck, the pool sparkled like a piece of turquoise, with facets of flickering gold where my father chiseled at the surface. Overhead, the glass ceiling reflected the dancing underlit water.

My mother and I sat down on recliners and swaddled ourselves in motel bath towels.

Then my father climbed out of the pool and went over to the diving board, stared down at the water. We knew what he was doing—sizing up the deep end, planning how his outstretched praying hands would pave the way. He pinched water out of his nose, ran his hand over his head. This will be a good one, is what we knew he was thinking.

He grabbed the metal railing and pulled himself up, standing stooped, as rigid as the board. He was going to do it, all right.

"Daddy, I wish you wouldn't," I said.

"Oh, hell," he said, giving the board a good bounce. "Quit worrying about me."

He walked to the end, looked over the edge.

"Gus," my mother said, putting her foot down.

But my father would not be stopped. He stepped back, then took two skipping steps forward, and slipped. His layout was not perfect, not even very good. I held my breath. A bellysmacker is what he did. Every inch of his rigid body fell against the sheet of water. I watched the surface break open and swallow him whole. The curtain of fallout illumined by the floodlights rained down on the Pink Flamingo bath towels.

On the way down, I think my father gasped.

Poolside, we waited.

"Gus?"

"Daddy?"

*

Years later we waited beside his hospital bed. It was dark except for the soft fluorescent light above his chart. We listened to him breathe, the long and the short of it. We waited out the in between, willed the tumble of air to return.

"Gus?"

"Daddy?"

We matched our breath to his. Every time he inhaled, paused, we wondered *this time?* Then he gasped, and I thought of him in the pool at the Pink Flamingo Motel, in the deep end, showing off.

MR. DOOLITTLE

The dogs want to lick my skin. Even the mongrels come running with sloppy, drooling tongues of affection. And the cats—they can't wait to knead on me with their softly-padded paws like I'm a doughy pillow that would rise just for them. Birds smash against the picture window thinking I'm available on the other side. Snakes sidle onto the burning sidewalk for my benefit, soaking up the intense heat until I come along and step gingerly over them, sending the languid ropes slithering into cooling grass. Those animals in the zoo—don't even get me started. When I walk through the gates peacocks pulsate their plumage, sea lions clap and dive, sloths start spinning excitedly, and bats in the bat exhibit have already echolocated my whereabouts: they sweep frantically in the dark waiting for me to arrive, the light of their day.

And you?

You stand by a tree gazing into your glowing phone, neck bent, ears keen on multitasking: somehow you know it's me when I walk into your personal space—maybe I cast a shadow over your precious screen. You don't look, flick your eyebrows and say, "What's up?" and when you follow me across the park to the picnic table a mosquito lands on my skin. I don't slap her away. I let her suck my blood. She needs it to make her eggs. Her prick stings just a little. It's a small price to pay. I'm hoping she'll land on you next, our blood comingling in her belly. I'll bet you don't know only female mosquitoes drink blood. Google it, it's true.

ANOTHER LIFE

Flying along US Highway 31, we're listening to "Appalachian Spring" blare through the speakers. Marla's my slumped passenger, seatbelt unbuckled.

"I'm just saying it'd be better," she says, staring out the window. "Kiss the family's butt. And I wouldn't have to worry about someone dying 'cause they're already dead."

We're going to Interlochen. Marla's crazy about Aaron Copeland. Some youth orchestra's playing "Appalachian Spring" and "Fanfare for the Common Man." Marla scored us two free tickets.

"Then do it," I say, nudging up the AC.

I keep my eyes trained on the tree line. Deer thick as gnats in these parts. Never hit one yet. But there's always a *yet* lurking somewhere. I feel it like the hairs on the back of my neck, keep my hands 10 and 2.

Marla's in one of her moods. "Hey, you mind if I smoke?"

I do, but I'm crazy about Marla. "Be my guest."

She rolls down the window. "And regular hours. No nightshift. No more 16-hour days."

"Go for it."

You know how many shades of green in a Michigan forest? Almost as many as in Marla's deep-set, thick-lashed eyes.

In another life—a *previous* life—Marla was a flapper. Bobbed hair. Jazz lover. Maybe Isadora Duncan. Swears she sometimes wakes up with the feeling of silk around her neck.

Once, I woke up to the scent of roses. I smelled them the rest of the day no matter where I went. Marla said a spirit came to visit me. The next day I got a sinus infection. I never told Marla: Best to let her think what she wants.

Wind whips her bottle-blonde hair like octopus legs. On her, messy hair looks better than good. She blows clouds of gray out the window. Marla is one person who actually looks good smoking. Like she was made for it.

"And here's the best part," she says between drags. "There's a funeral home two blocks from the house. I'll never be late. And black. I look good in *black*. At least I think so."

"Of course you do."

Two days ago Marla had a patient "die on her"—that's how she refers to death, like the patient had a say in the outcome and chose to involve Marla. The guy was only twenty-two, a college graduate, blue-green eyes Nurse Marla couldn't help but notice. His end was expected, but Marla wasn't expecting it to come on her shift. These things, these awful, sad things she has to handle.

"Well, I can't go back to that fucking hospital." She tosses the butt out the window.

We talk about going back—or not. I'm not going back to teach at the college except when I have to—due bills, past-due bills—which is in another week.

Interlochen is a town in northern Michigan. It's also the name of a fine arts school where Marla thinks she should have gone back in the day. Really, Marla is a dancer trapped in a nurse's body. She's got lithe limbs and a strong torso and cuts a nice line when she graces the floor. But she's got to have something in her veins to get her bare feet moving. Last night at the bar her feet had too many. She fell off the table. Bar-types will never appreciate a good jitterbug.

"Pull off here," she says, pointing at a rest stop. I thread the car down the ramp, pull beside a jack pine. Two rigs are parked in the semi lot. It's useless to try to get Marla to ignore them. "I'll be right back," she says and marches off. I cut the engine, get out and walk to the vending machines. Two of the three—out of order. I drop quarters, wait for my cup of coffee. The cup drops lopsided. I reach in to straighten it and hot coffee drips on my hand. Before I can stifle myself, "Ouch, fucking dammit!" pours out.

A woman in overalls and a tube top comes around the corner. I'd recognize a lot lizard anywhere. This one has more than a forked-tongue, but turns out she's nice. She comes back from the restroom with a couple of wet paper towels for my hand.

"Thanks," I tell her politely.

She drops quarters in the slot, points at some words on the machine. *"Warning: Coffee is hot. Not liable for damages incurred from this machine."* She grins, pulls a cup of hot cocoa from the holding bay. "I'm just yankin' your rope. It don't actually say that. Ya gonna be okay?"

I tell her I'm fine and watch her walk out to the shiny red-fleck cab. Just then Marla comes out of the restroom, lips painted fresh burgundy, hair pulled back in a scrunchie, beaming.

Back in the car, she waits until we're on the highway, rolls down her window, lights the joint. "Did I ever tell you about Paris in the 20's? How I met Hemingway and Fitzgerald?"

She taps my shoulder, holds out the joint.

What the hell? I think. I don't want to cough my ass off while I'm driving so I take a small drag. The smoke burns, and then floats away.

Not another car on this two-lane road as far as the eye can see. Pine, birch, pine, birch, *pine-pine-pine*—we're flying past these evergreens—*ever*—green—and they're doing nothing but being noticed. Trees, I so envy them. Covered with snow, they'll be beautiful come winter.

BUTTON, BUTTON

I lose things. Last week I lost my car—then found it, parked in a row I swore was not mine. Today it was a button. A thin disk of mother-of-pearl, standard issue: two holes. My theory—one of the holes was sharp, sent that way from the factory. My fingers worked the fragile thread against the eyelet. One loop set free—the rest, history.

Had I paid more attention, seen its concave body sag, I'd have gotten needle and thread and tied it off with a good solid knot.

Or not.

My mother tried to teach me, but I refused to learn. Her fingers were nimble from pounding keyboards all those years at the General Electric. Years later, watching television, she'd air-type O-x-y-d-o-l. Or P-i-n-e-s-o-l. Even as she lay dying, the synapses fired away, digits dancing to a silent tune.

Typing was a skill to fall back on; I fell into it. In school, I learned on manual keyboards. *Asdf, asdf. Now is the time for all good men.*

I was good. Not as good, but almost. In class, when the teacher wasn't looking, I typed letters I never sent. I still do. I write, *Remember the coat you got me, the one I wouldn't wear?* I mention the button and when my fingers find the keys I type: *Button, button—who's got the button? That's* what I'd like to know. And what comes next—after the question, I mean.

AT THE BEACH

The parking lot is crowded when they pull in. In the distance, the sun begins its descent behind a curtain of wispy clouds.

When water roils, in seagulls and plovers retreat to dry sand, but when it recedes they rush like jay-walkers to the glistening surface, picking off lake flies and dead minnows.

The sun is a pink iris closing on a dappled blue-black sky.

Rest assured the world will come to an apocryphal end. But don't count your chickens before they hatch.

"I want a good tan," the girl with the parrot tattoo on her shoulder says, laying her blanket out just so.

In other years they would not mind the trouble that has come to them, they would have outrun it as easily as if they'd turned a corner onto the darkest street in town.

Beach detritus: crumpled Mylar balloons, pink and yellow ribbon, cracked plastic cups, a wine cork.

He said: If you'd seen them run into the lake like that you'd have wondered if they hadn't been raised in a barn.

Out on the horizon where water meets sky—Wisconsin.

Cone-suckers lean against the warm bodies of cars, engines still pinging. They lick waffle cones mounded over with ice cream— Blue Moon, Eskimo Kisses, Caramel Caribou, Mackinac Island Fudge. There are other flavors at House of Flavors, but the couple stormed out with grease still glistening on their fingertips. "That's all I'm saying," he pleaded after her.

There, can you see it over there?

Sunsets are a big deal in a tourist town. Everybody comes to this beach on Lake Michigan.

Forget the seagulls and plovers. They've already had their fill of the horizon.

MUSEUM PIECES

If you ask me, the babies are the thing to see. Sure, the vintage W.W. II German submarine is a rare treat—and it's partially submerged so that looking out the port holes it's real water you're seeing! But the sub isn't so great if you suffer from claustrophobia, as I do.

There's the walk-out aquarium, offering a spectacular underwater view of Lake Michigan. The star of the show is a great white who likes to surprise his leering visitors—he charges like a missile, then swerves before ramming the Plexiglas partition. If you ask me he's nothing compared to those little jaundiced wonders.

No, for my money the babies are tops, and if you go to the museum any day but the weekend—when all the yappy, snot-nosed kids come to visit—you can gaze at these miniature miracles for as long as you'd like. You can even count their teeny fingers and tiny toes till your heart's content!

The other day I went to see the sweet, forever-dreaming babies. It was Monday, a free day, though I would have gladly paid full price. I hurried in, bypassing the Hall of Electricity, the Exploration of Space Exhibit, the Real Working Coal Mine. I found my way to where they were mounted and ran my finger over the cool glass. It was early, the museum had just opened. The chambers were still fingerprint- and smudge-free. There was a whole series of babies, a regular gallery, and I went to the last one first; I mean, the one with legs and arms and ears in place. He had a smirk on his golden face, as if to say, *I told you so*. He squeezed his hands into tiny fists and floated, suspended in a sea of formaldehyde. His eyes were closed, naturally.

I started with him because he was the one that mattered—although that baby with the gills for lungs always caught my eye. The dot of conception, no bigger than the head of a needle, the first "baby," I always breezed right past.

Only once did I start at the beginning, and that was when I didn't go alone. We moved right along, pointing to this one and that. "See how it looks at six weeks, eight weeks, fifteen weeks old!" I said, sounding like a well-trained docent. I looked lovingly at the babies; the babies looked lovingly back.

I read each plaque aloud.

"At sixteen weeks," I said. But only one of us was listening. "What's the point?" he said, and I said, Education. The point was Education. Where else could we see what our lives could have looked like, spelled out like a jigsaw puzzle?

He said, "You're crazy, you know that. Out of your fucking mind."

I said did he know that by the end of the fourth month eyebrows and lashes are formed?

"Shut up," he said. "For Christ's sake, shut up."

After we got home, I remembered something else I was going to show him—my other favorite thing at the museum: the Whispering Chamber. It's a long, dark hall. At one end is a Plexiglas wall the shape of a praying hand, and directly opposite, thirty or forty feet away, is its mate. In the middle of the room is nothing but dark, cool space, the kind you don't want to leave. This is how it works: you put your feet on the footprints painted on the floor, and into that nice big hand you whisper your secrets. The person standing next to you can't hear a thing. Still, your secrets take flight, travel to the far end of the darkened room, and land at the feet of a total stranger.

PAPER CUP

It's early morning in the natatorium. He watches her swim laps, long fingers cupping handfuls of gorgeous turquoise water, long dark hair trailing in the wake. Illumined by the glow of the underwater lights her pale skin pulls him under. He imagines the two of them swimming, sees her strong arms reaching out to him instead of the other end of the pool. He extends a hand, touches one of her solid thighs. Her flesh is smooth and cool as the underbelly of a fish. They bob up and down in the gentle waves.

It's break time. He's drinking coffee, earthy Sumatra. Already he's checked the pool for contamination, added chlorine, mopped the deck, swabbed down the plastic chairs and loungers—all SOP. On Thursdays, "her day," he hurries to get his work done so he can sit and watch. Watch and sip. When his paper cup isn't touching his lips his nostrils detect locker room mold. It's always there; he carries it home with him in his pores at the end of the day. Emanating from his rough workman's hands is a musky scent of worn off years, time shed in orifices. When no one's looking he sniffs like a dog trying to track her. After she leaves the natatorium he'll put the "Cleaning" sign on the locker room door and go in. He could find anything: a long strand of black hair, a smudge of talc, a tissue besotted with pink lip gloss—any and all of it potentially hers, and he tucks it all away inside his dark pockets.

She's half way across the pool. The water in her lane, electrified. Her arms cleave the crystal surface, her feet kick without splash like a ballerina's plait done over and over. In swimmer's parlance, she's punishing the water. He would gladly dive to the bottom of the pool, near the hair-infested drain pipe, just to watch her swim above him.

His hand shakes. He squeezes the paper cup. For now he's here watching her there. But someday soon he will find a way to reach out and make her see. Can't she see? My God, he's been here in the shadows so long, biding his time. A maintenance man maintaining.

Someday her shapely arms will reach out to him. When they do, he will never let her go.

EN PLEIN AIR

A woman with no apparent artistic skills signed up for a plein air workshop at the local senior citizens center. The instructor, a man in his early fifties, a school bus driver by day, had the small group of neophyte artists set up their easels in a well-manicured area next to the parking lot.

For three of the four weeks the weather had been perfect— October blessed them with a beautiful Indian summer. Elms and maples across the street were robust reds, yellows and oranges. By the third week, warm winds shook loose their colorful bounty. Spectacular leaves bright as a parrot's plumage fluttered to the ground and the artists dabbed and daubed furiously to capture the moment.

Even the woman with no artistic skills made a respectable showing, covering her canvas with rich unmuddied hues. Still, her subject matter left something to the imagination. Her sky seemed lifeless and one-dimensional, and the trunk of her birch appeared toothpick flimsy, a few of its branches hairy spider legs instead of limbs. Yet when her fellow painters looked at her canvas they nodded approvingly, understanding it to be a tree.

On the last class, students stared off into deep space then back at their canvases. Leaves drunkenly tumbled as if they couldn't hit the ground fast enough. Winds rifled through the treetops. Fluffy clouds turned dark and foreboding as if Titian's brush was furiously at work. The storm blew in fast. An ominous funnel cloud descended on the senior center, panicking the budding artists who abandoned their projects and dashed inside.

Aggressive winds overturned wobbly wooden easels and swept up the colorful canvases like kites tethered to fraying strings. The wet paintings were carelessly tossed across the senior center's parking lot.

All but one canvas was ruined—that which had been painted by the woman with no artistic skills. At the last moment, as a mother would take a child by the hand and run for safety, she had grabbed her precious canvas off the easel and carried it into the building.

In the storm's aftermath, the thin birch she had been painting was the only tree left standing. The stout maples and resistive elms had all been snapped cleanly in half.

E-BOOK DISCUSSION QUESTIONS (A SAMPLE)

1.   Story collections like *The Forest for the Trees* were once printed on paper pages and bound into books rather than read as e-books on the screen. If the eight stories in *The Forest for the Trees* were printed on real paper, what kind of deciduous and/or coniferous trees would be used for each story? Why that particular tree and not another? If borer weevils infested the trees, would that affect the plot, character or setting of the story?

2.   If Dick in "How It All Went Down" married Sally in "Open Hearts," and if Sally had had a transgendered child (which is alluded to in "Open Hearts"), what might that child have been named—and would he/she have had black or blonde hair, and in what way might hair color have affected the outcome of Dick and Sally's relationship (assuming Dick knows nothing about Sally's prior arrest for racketeering)?

3.   If the viola that Jill plays in "A Day at the Symphony" were instead an electric 6-string Gibson guitar with Grover Milk Bottle Rotomatic tuners and Burstbucker 1&2 pickups, would Jill have continued seeing Bill, meeting him in clandestine chambers—and would she still have orgasms? Furthermore, what might this story be saying about the affairs of musicians in general, and violists in particular?

4.   The theme of parental love is predominate in *The Forest for the Trees*. In what way can you relate to the relationship of the mother and daughter in "Green Car, Green Light," and what do you think would have happened if Sheila, the master gardener in "Daffodils and Owls" had chosen to have a child before she was thirty years old instead of adopting the Asian child with her lover, Gladdis? Can people ever find happiness from their actions, and should stories and fiction in general be pressed to answer to anything, especially to wine-drinking book clubs whose members don't really give a shit what happens and who, the day after book club, forget what it was they said and didn't say and meant to say?

SOME NUMBERS

This is your telephone—not a stylish retro, but a relic rotary, a "space saver."

In the center of the dial is an old area code: 219. Today, if you dial 219, you will reach someone in northwest Indiana, someone who lives in Gary, Hobart, Whiting, Crown Point, or Hammond. For a long time, 219 was the area code for your hometown, which is due east of Gary, Hobart, Whiting, Crown Point, Hammond—on the other side of Indiana. Now your area code is 260, though sometimes your fingers still retain a 2-1-9 memory.

Beneath the dial is a chunky, black, hard-bodied trunk, with a faded yellow label that contains four telephone numbers: one for Time and Temp, one for the Market Line, one for Emergency, and one for something called the Fun Line. For kicks, you dial the Fun Line, but end up getting a busy tone.

Your phone is a great conversation piece. Like the time not long ago when a repairman who had come to the house noticed your antique rotary on the wall. He was waiting for you to write him a check. "Wow, cool phone," he said. "Does it even work?"

"Yes," you said, "Try it."

He might have hefted the receiver had his cell phone not begun to sound off, some blaring, bump-and-jive ringtone. He excused himself, went outside to take the call. You, on the other hand, may not leave or wander around; you must stand in one place. Your rotary phone with its coiled black cord tethers you there.

Like the time when your mother began to die on the grass verge after the two of you had come home from the cemetery. Somewhere between the cemetery and home, your mother couldn't catch her breath. She gasped for air. It was a beautiful spring day, the air crisp. Your mother collapsed on the verge, and you ran into the house, straight to that wall-bound rotary and yanked the receiver off and didn't even have to look at the Emergency number—911, 911, 911. But you dialed 1-1-9.

Because you were flustered and afraid? Because you were certain your mother was going to die in the shade of an old maple tree? You didn't need to look at the number on the label because you knew the number. *Everyone* knows the number.

You dialed 1-1-9.

There isn't an operational 119 prefix in the telephone world that you know. Not even a 119 area code in the United States.

There is a 119 country code for New Zealand.

New Zealand is more than 8,000 miles from Indiana, about as far from you as that day your mother began to die on the verge.

You are numerically dyslexic. In college, when your German professor told the class to turn to *Seite funf und vierzig* (page five and forty, or forty-five), you turned to page fifty-four and sat there confused.

Your mother did not die that day, the day you dialed 119. Nor did she die the next day or the next. It was a week later, in the hospital. After she drew her last breath, they closed the curtain around her bed and escorted you across the hall into an empty room so they could "take care of some things." You sat in the dark, fingers twisted, wondering what things you yourself would now need to take care of.

Later, you went home to that empty house and sat at the desk staring at your rotary phone, at its coiled cord, twisted and dangling. You saw the black numbers printed in the center of the white dial: area code 219, and your telephone number—some 2s, a 4, a 6, some 8s. It's the same number you have today. Only the area code, 260, has changed.

YOUR HEARTBEAT

In a state where prickly arms of Ponderosa pine wave their welcome,

In a county honoring a dead Indian chief whose name you
can't pronounce,

In a town where folks flash waxen smiles and cut strangers
with side glances,

In a motel owned and operated by an old man named Patel,

In a room, 4B, embalmed with cigarette smoke from years gone by,

In a bed that vibrates to a handful of quarters,

In a heart ready to jettison a payload of remorse and guilt,

In a chamber where lust once dwelled,

In a rush of mad intoxicated blood,

In a single, negligible contracting cell,

I'll be there and you'll never even know.

THE ODYSSEY

Shit happens. A woman grows older and wiser and pretty soon she's doing a lot of thinking—the kind that can happen anywhere: washing dishes, folding laundry, pushing a vacuum.

One day she's watching TV—but not really. She's thinking. Another time she's driving to the store deep in thought, not paying attention to the streetlights.

A few days later she's in her car, driving west. Illinois isn't so different from Indiana. Iowa sort of looks like Illinois. And then—Montana. Big Sky country. Lovely, but big. Soon she's in California, dipping her toes in the Pacific. She doesn't like the ocean or "the ocean life" and all the bums and weirdoes who cling to it like barnacles.

Still, here she is. The last frontier. The farthest sunset in America (if you don't count Hawaii).

Every evening she has a glass of wine with her meals. Soon she dispenses with the glass and drinks her vino straight from the bottle (saves on dishes). One night she looks in the mirror: she's older and lonelier.

She joins a bicycle club. The club meets on Thursday evenings. They take short scenic tours, but mostly they do it for the wine after the rides. By the time she pedals back to her condo she's crocked. Doesn't care. She's met someone. Someone nice. Someone she can talk to, someone who seems to like the same things she likes.

The next day this person calls. She answers on the second ring (doesn't want to appear too anxious). They agree to meet for coffee and dessert. She goes out and buys herself a new outfit, up-styles herself with the competent help of a young sales woman whose nose-ring she can't help but admire.

That night at the coffee shop they drink espresso. Order thick slices of cheesecake. Talk. Laugh. They have so much in common!

At night's end they agree to meet again and then kiss awkwardly in the parking lot, which leads to one thing and another. The next morning she wakes in a strange bed. She drags herself to the bathroom and looks in the mirror. Creases and lines, wrinkles and gray hair: still there.

In her sagging belly she knows the relationship won't work. Like she knows the back of her own hand (before it got wrinkly and spotted with age).

The next day she joins a tennis club. Hasn't played in years. Surprisingly her game comes back to her with relative ease. Like riding a bicycle. She places shots at will, though her serve is rusty. They play a set. The ball clips the sideline. She stretches but knows she will never reach it. Knows in the pit of her stomach her old arthritic knees are rebelling. She doesn't even try to make the shot. It's the first time she's ever relented. Remembers years ago, when she was young, playing with older players who gave up on shots and it drove her crazy. Now, she understands.

That evening from her balcony she watches a fat orange sun dip beneath the water's edge. An economy-sized jug of Merlot keeps her company. Here she is, the last frontier. She still despises the ocean and all it stands for. And as the sun sets, her hands appear more like the ones she used to know.

JACKPOT

At the Amoco station a man slouched inside the booth, his posture telling me he planned to be there a while. Across the street, at Texaco, a woman and child huddled together inside a Plexiglas booth, the woman's hands flying the whole time, deep into something; she gave me a hard look, as if to say, Get your own damn phone. So I turned around and got in my car and drove to the mall, where there were three pay-phones next to the Food Court alone. A yeasty smell wafted over from Hot Sam's and a juicer masticated fresh fruit at the Orange Julius stand. I went to the last booth, nearest the restrooms, where it was quiet and pleasantly smelled of disinfectant. Before feeding a coin into the gaping slot, I noticed a cleaning lady who had come out of the restroom. My heart went out to her. She was heavy, her ankles thick. She reminded me of my own sweet mother.

I dropped the coin, examined names and numbers scratched into the enamel—a pimpled surface painted over so many times I could chip away and carry off a rainbow of color beneath my fingernail. Soon I would hear my mother's voice— low, nasal, reassuring—reaching across the distance and as always she'd take her time. Hel-lo, she'd say, emphasizing both syllables. Mesmerized, I would be content to stand there all day listening to her lilting voice through the wires—Hel-lo, hel-lo—imprinting the inflection, the tone, the pitch to memory. A true perfectionist, she took I don't know how many times to get the message just right. I had given her the machine the Christmas before. "Why do I need this?" she had said, laughing as she tugged it from the box, but I could tell she was thrilled to get it.

The coin slid through the pay phone, exiting out the chute as if I'd hit the jackpot. I fished it out and sent it back down again, and this time I remembered my uncle's old slot machine, the one he had won in a poker game. Whenever we went over to his house I was allowed to go to the basement to play the one-armed bandit while he and my parents visited. My uncle always kept a Chase and Sanborn coffee can filled with dimes to last an unlucky gambler all night long. Sometimes my mother would come down and join me. Every now and then a row of bright red cherries would roll over and she'd cry "Bingo!" as if she were in some smoky American Legion Hall instead of her brother's damp and dreary basement. "Mom," I'd correct her, "it's *jackpot.*"

But she didn't care. She was happy to have hit upon a little luck any way she could—which was exactly how I felt standing there, listening to her tell me she couldn't come to the phone right now, but to go ahead and leave a message.

Of course, I didn't. And just what might I have said? That I missed her? That I wished we could talk, like before? Instead, I hung up. And then I went to my car and started home, and as I was driving across town I realized it was about time I finally unplugged her answering machine and got serious about selling her house. After all, she'd been gone for months now and all that time I'd had to listen to her promise to get back to me as soon as possible—the only promise I'd ever known her not to keep.

Ds Levy has worked as a tennis instructor, magazine editor, copywriter, and college professor. A graduate of the Bennington Writing Seminars, she has been a recipient of several Individual Artist grants from the Indiana Arts Commission. She has had work published in the *Alaska Quarterly Review, Columbia, Little Fiction, Brevity, The Pinch, The Common, Glimmer Train*, and others. In 2016 she received a Pushcart Prize nomination for fiction. She and her husband, their dog and cats live in Indiana and northern Michigan.

CPSIA information can be obtained
at www.ICGtesting.com
Printed in the USA
BVHW082253250319
543600BV00003B/297/P